Female FOODIES

Peggy Cherng
Panda Express Empress

Rebecca Felix

Checkerboard Library

An Imprint of Abdo Publishing
abdopublishing.com

abdopublishing.com

Published by Abdo Publishing, a division of ABDO, PO Box 398166, Minneapolis, Minnesota 55439. Copyright © 2018 by Abdo Consulting Group, Inc. International copyrights reserved in all countries. No part of this book may be reproduced in any form without written permission from the publisher. Checkerboard Library™ is a trademark and logo of Abdo Publishing.

Printed in the United States of America, North Mankato, Minnesota
102017
012018

THIS BOOK CONTAINS
RECYCLED MATERIALS

Design: Sarah DoYoung, Mighty Media, Inc.
Production: Mighty Media, Inc.
Editor: Liz Salzmann
Cover Photographs: Alamy; Mighty Media, Inc.
Interior Photographs: Alamy, pp. 9, 15, 19, 23; Bev Sykes/Flickr, p. 21; Candy Beauchamp/Flickr, p. 17; Getty Images, p. 27; iStockphoto, pp. 7, 13, 28 (bottom), 29 (top); Shutterstock, pp. 11, 28 (top), 29 (bottom)
Background Pattern: Shutterstock, cover, pp. 3, 5, 7, 9, 11, 13, 15, 17, 19, 21, 23, 27, 31

Publisher's Cataloging-in-Publication Data
Names: Felix, Rebecca, author.
Title: Peggy Cherng: Panda Express empress / by Rebecca Felix.
Other titles: Panda Express empress
Description: Minneapolis, Minnesota : Abdo Publishing, 2018. | Series: Female foodies |
    Includes online resources and index.
Identifiers: LCCN 2017944027 | ISBN 9781532112669 (lib.bdg.) | ISBN 9781532150388 (ebook)
Subjects: LCSH: Cherng, Peggy, 1948-.--Juvenile literature. | Businesswomen--United States--Biography--
    Juvenile literature. | Fast food restaurants--Juvenile literature. | Entrepreneurship--Juvenile
    literature.
Classification: DDC 338.76647 [B]--dc23
LC record available at https://lccn.loc.gov/2017944027

Contents

Chapter 1

Panda Powerhouse

You're shopping at the mall with friends and decide to get some lunch. The food court has many restaurants. But there really isn't a choice to make. You and your friends always go to Panda Express. It's everyone's favorite.

Your mouth waters as you wait in line. One of the staff scoops steaming fried rice and **wok**-tossed Orange Chicken into bowls. You can already almost taste the Orange Chicken's famous **tangy** sauce!

Panda Express is a **chain** of American Chinese restaurants. It serves traditional Chinese food with changes made to appeal to American tastes. Panda Express is the largest Chinese food chain in the United States. It has nearly 2,000 restaurants! These restaurants are owned and overseen by two people.

Peggy and Andrew Cherng are the people behind Panda Express. The husband and wife are both co-**chair** and co-**CEO** of the company Panda Restaurant Group. In addition to Panda Express, the company owns Panda Inn

Peggy Cherng is one of the most successful Chinese-American businesswomen.

and Hibachi-San restaurants. Panda Restaurant Group began as one small restaurant run by Andrew and his father. Peggy joined the business shortly after they started opening more locations. She is credited with shaping it into the successful **chain** it is today.

Chapter 2
American Education

Peggy Tsiang was born around 1950 in Burma, a Southeast Asian nation known today as Myanmar. When Peggy was young, her family moved to Hong Kong. As a teenager, Peggy came to the United States to attend Baker University in Baldwin City, Kansas. There, Peggy studied mathematics.

Andrew Cherng was born in China in 1948. He moved to Japan in 1963. Three years later, he moved to the United States to attend Baker University. That is where Andrew and Peggy met. The pair bonded over their Chinese roots and love of math. They started dating.

After completing **bachelor's degrees**, Andrew and Peggy continued their education. Both attended the University of Missouri. There, Andrew earned a

Food Bite

Food in the United States was a big surprise to Peggy. She had never had pizza or tacos before!

The University of Missouri is in Columbia, Missouri.

master's degree in math. Peggy earned a master's degree in computer science.

Peggy stayed in school after earning her master's degree. She went on to earn a **PhD** in electrical **engineering**. Meanwhile, Andrew began a new venture that would completely change his and Peggy's lives.

Chapter 3

California Careers

Andrew's cousin had a restaurant in California called Ting Ho. In 1972, he asked Andrew to help him run it. Andrew was familiar with restaurant operations. During college, he had spent his holiday breaks waiting tables. And Andrew's father, Ming-Tsai Cherng, was a chef.

Andrew moved to California and began working at Ting Ho. But soon, he and his cousin began to disagree about how to run the business. Andrew decided he wanted his own restaurant. By this time, much of Andrew's family had moved to the United States. Andrew asked his father to help him open a restaurant.

On June 8, 1973, the two opened Panda Inn in Pasadena, California. Panda Inn was a full-service American Chinese restaurant. Ming-Tsai cooked the food. Andrew ran the dining area. Money was tight at first. Several family

Food Bite

In China, the panda is a symbol of friendship and peace.

During school breaks, Andrew worked at Chinese restaurants in New York City.

members worked in the restaurant for no pay. But Andrew was sure the restaurant would soon be a success.

Peggy earned her **PhD** in 1974. The next year, she and Andrew married and she took his last name. Cherng moved to California. She worked at **aerospace** company McDonnell Douglas. There, Cherng designed computer systems. She had no idea this work would one day help revolutionize the Cherng family restaurant business.

Chapter 4

Family and Business

Cherng worked at McDonnell Douglas until 1977. That year, she took an engineering job at Comtal-3M. She also managed the company's **software** department. As Cherng's career experience grew, so did her and Andrew's family. The couple welcomed three daughters in the late 1970s and early 1980s. They named their children Andrea, Nicole, and Michelle.

The Cherngs became busy working parents. As Cherng created computer systems at her job, Andrew and his father enjoyed success with Panda Inn. Andrew had dreams of growing the business. He told his mother his goal was to open 100 restaurants in the future!

In the early 1980s, Andrew set his goal in motion. In 1982, he opened a Panda Inn in Glendale, California. Around that time, he was introduced to Dan Donahue.

Food Bite

Andrew's mother told him, "You only eat three meals a day. What do you need 100 restaurants for?"

Today, the Panda Express sign is a common sight in food courts around the world.

Donahue was in charge of building the Glendale Galleria mall. Donahue asked Andrew if he would like to open a restaurant in the food court at the mall. Andrew said yes.

Unfortunately, Andrew's father was not alive to see the business grow. Ming-Tsai had died in 1981. Both the family and its restaurants felt the loss greatly. It was due to both this loss and the expansion plans that Cherng joined the family business.

Chapter 5

New Developments

Cherng quit her job at Comtal-3M to work with her husband in 1982. In October 1983, the new restaurant opened in the Glendale Galleria. It was a fast food **version** of the Panda Inn, called Panda Express. The menu offered a smaller selection and the food was prepared more quickly.

As Andrew got the restaurant running, Cherng saw a way to use her **software** expertise. She felt a software system could make the restaurant more organized. Cherng set up a software system called Panda **Automated** Work Stations at Panda Express. It was nicknamed PAWS.

PAWS kept track of orders and other records. The system also kept track of **inventory**. When an ingredient ran low, the software automatically ordered more. At the time, it was the only Chinese restaurant that used computers.

PAWS revolutionized the way Panda Express did business. It helped the employees be more productive. In 1985, the couple opened a Panda Express in the Westside Pavilion mall in Los Angeles, California. By the end of that year, they had nine restaurants.

Today, Panda Express employs 27,000 people in its restaurants around the world!

Chapter 6
Fresh Take

The Cherngs' restaurants were doing well. Peggy Cherng has been called the "secret ingredient" that led Panda Express to increased growth and success. Her systems kept costs down so the business had more money to expand.

It was tricky to prepare and serve quality Chinese dishes quickly. But the Cherngs found a way to master it. The key to their success was preparation and presentation.

Every location had an open kitchen. Customers could see the food being prepared. Also within sight was a large cooler holding fresh vegetables. Finally, a steam table kept dishes hot, ready-to-serve, and visible to customers as they ordered. These elements gave customers the impression the food was always fresh.

Cherng's **software** proved to be a great tool for this type of service. The system not only kept track of **inventory**, it also recorded shifts in consumer behavior. This way, Cherng was able to see what dishes were and weren't selling. This data showed what customers wanted, so the restaurants could focus on the most popular dishes.

Panda Express staff check the temperature of the food three times a day to make sure it is kept hot enough.

Chapter 7
Chicken Winner

Diners had come to expect the same quality dishes at each Panda Express. Several items became customer favorites. But it was the **chain's** Orange Chicken that became its **signature** dish.

Chicken was a main ingredient in many Panda Express dishes. Chicken has two types of meat, white and dark. Studies have shown that most US consumers prefer white meat. Because of this, many restaurants only serve white meat chicken. But in Asia, the dark meat is more popular. Cherng wanted to prepare it in a way Americans would enjoy.

In 1987, Panda Express chef Andy Kao came up with the solution. He created a new dish by frying battered, boneless pieces of dark meat. The batter became crisp on the outside while keeping the meat juicy inside. Kao covered these

Food Bite

Panda Express restaurants served 67.9 million pounds (30.8 million kg) of Orange Chicken in 2014.

The flavors of the Orange Chicken sauce were based on flavors used in classic dishes of the Hunan province in China.

crispy pieces of chicken in a special orange sauce. The sauce has been **described** as equal parts sweet, spicy, sour, and **tangy**. Orange Chicken was born.

Orange Chicken was an instant hit with Panda Express customers. Diners didn't seem to either notice or care that the dish was made with dark meat. They just thought it tasted great! Within five years, it was the top-selling Panda Express dish.

Chapter 8

CEO and Community

Panda Express continued to expand. By 1992, there were 97 Panda Express locations. Until 1988, Panda Express restaurants were located only in malls. That year, the **chain** started opening stores in **supermarkets**. In the following years, the couple also opened stand-alone locations.

Andrew handled getting the new stores up and running. Then Cherng took over. She trained the staff on her **software** system and made sure things ran smoothly. In 1990, Cherng became Panda Express **CEO**. Soon after, she was made company co-**chair**, sharing the title with Andrew.

The Cherngs opened more shops throughout the 1990s, and in new types of locations. These included airports and sports stadiums. The one-hundredth store opened in 1993.

In 1997, Cherng was named president and CEO of Panda Restaurant Group. Giving back to the community was very important to Cherng. So, in 1999, she established Panda Cares. This is a branch of the company that works to help children. Panda Cares promotes children's health and education. It also provides **disaster** relief.

Tom Davin (*right*) was CEO from 2004 to 2009. During this time, Cherng focused more on Panda Cares.

Chapter 9

Global Growth

Cherng and her husband proved they make a great team. And the couple was not done expanding their business. In 2003, they released a line of Panda Express sauces, sold in stores. In 2007, the company opened its one-thousandth Panda Express. It is located in Pasadena, California.

One of the Cherngs' goals is to have at least one Panda Express in each US state. By 2017, there were locations in 48 states. Only Vermont and New Hampshire had no Panda Express locations.

The Panda Express empire extends outside the United States as well. The first international Panda Express opened in Mexico City, Mexico, in 2011. Locations in Canada, Puerto Rico, and South Korea followed. And the couple plans to open 250 more locations in Mexico by 2021.

Food Bite

The Cherngs entered the California Restaurant Association Hall of Fame in 2005.

YOU ARE ADMIRED FOR YOUR ADVENTUROUS WAYS

PANDA EXPRESS • PANDA INN

PANDA EXPRESS

GOURMET CHINESE FOOD

Experience P

Panda Express restaurants hand out $1 million worth of fortune cookies each month.

Some people don't understand how the Cherngs run so many restaurants themselves. Many restaurant **chains franchise** their businesses. Having different owners running new locations can help a chain grow faster.

But Cherng and Andrew feel Panda Express grows quickly enough. They also feel they have been successful at overseeing all the locations. They don't plan to change how they run the company.

Chapter 10

Above and Beyond

The Cherngs credit part of their success to their relationships with their employees. Cherng works to form strong relationships and support systems for Panda Express workers. The company calls its employees associates. They are also often referred to as Pandas. Cherng says Panda Restaurant Group's main goal is to be a company that creates happy Pandas. She believes happy associates lead to happy guests.

The company works hard to make sure each associate is satisfied with his or her job. Panda Restaurant Group associates are paid more than those employed at similar fast-service jobs. Panda Express workers enjoy other benefits as well. They get paid time off and can earn bonuses. The company also contributes to associates' retirement plans and education expenses.

Throughout their employment, associates are encouraged to grow and learn. The Cherngs focus on promoting from within the company. They train associates to take on more responsibility and earn higher positions if they wish.

Panda employees must commit to providing excellent customer service, and to continuing to learn while on the job.

Chapter 11

Recipe for Success

Getting to know their staff is very important to the Cherngs. Teaching them to make Panda Express food correctly is just as important. Cherng and Andrew oversee the training of their managers. This is to make sure each dish is prepared the same way every time, in every location.

To get this training, Panda Express managers visit the Panda Restaurant Group headquarters in Rosemead, California. There is a Panda Express restaurant inside the headquarters. It is used only for Panda manager training, which the Cherngs oversee.

Cherng and Andrew each have their own office at the headquarters. They sometimes have different opinions. But the couple's teamwork is key to their company's success. They each use their own strengths to keep the company strong.

Food Bite

Panda Express is ten times larger than its next largest fast-serve Chinese food competitor.

Peggy Cherng

By the Numbers

3

number of Panda Express stores built each week, as of 2006

7

number of countries in which Panda Express restaurants are located

48

number of US states in which Panda Express restaurants are located

17,000

number of Panda Express employees in 2008

27,000

number of Panda Express employees in 2017

67,900,900

pounds of Orange Chicken sold by Panda Express in 2014

2,800,000,000

amount in dollars the Panda Express **chain** made in sales in 2016

3,200,000,000

amount in dollars that Cherng and her husband were worth in 2017

Chapter 12

Cherng's Legacy

Peggy Cherng continues to lead the company in giving back to the community. In 2015, Panda Cares held a Family Day. For one day, Panda Express **donated** part of its sales to US food banks. Cherng and Andrew then matched that donation to double it. The money raised provided 10 million meals for US families in need.

The same year, *Nation's Restaurant News* named Cherng a Golden **Chain** winner for her leadership and generosity. In 2016, Cherng made *Forbes* magazine's list of American richest self-made women. Cherng also helps oversee other charities, as well a hospital and a management college.

But of all Cherng's earned titles and successes, she is proudest of the way Panda Express and its employees have grown. The example Cherng has set as a powerful female boss inspires

Food Bite

Forbes magazine listed Cherng's net worth in 2016 as $1.5 billion!

Cherng (*fourth from left*) and executives from other companies at the 2013 John Wooden Global Leadership Awards

her female employees, as well as her daughters. All three of Cherng's children have at times worked in the family business.

Cherng's **software** expertise and strong leadership helped turn Panda Express from two restaurants to nearly 2,000 stores. Thanks to Cherng, the **chain's** famous Orange Chicken and steaming rice are found around almost every corner!

Timeline

1950s

Peggy Tsiang is born in Burma, known today as Myanmar.

1960s

Peggy moves to the United States to attend college. She meets Andrew Cherng at Baker University in Kansas.

1975

Andrew and Peggy Cherng are married.

1982

Cherng joins her husband's restaurant business, applying software knowledge she has gained in her engineering career.

1990s

The Panda Express chain continues to grow, opening stand-alone locations and restaurants in airports and sports stadiums.

1973

Andrew and his father open Panda Inn in California.

1974

Peggy earns her PhD in electrical engineering from the University of Missouri.

1983

In October, the first Panda Express opens in Glendale Galleria mall in California.

1987

Panda Express chef Andy Kao creates Orange Chicken.

1999

Cherng establishes the company's charity branch, Panda Cares.

2011

Panda Express opens its first international location in Mexico City, Mexico

2016

Cherng is included in Forbes magazine's list of the country's richest self-made women.

Glossary

aerospace (EHR-oh-spays) – the space containing Earth's atmosphere and beyond. It is where rockets, satellites, and other spacecraft operate.

automated – able to move or act by itself. Something that is automated does things automatically.

bachelor's degree – a college degree usually earned after four years of study.

CEO – chief executive officer. The CEO is the person who makes the major decisions for running an organization or business.

chain – a group of businesses usually under a single ownership, management, or control.

chair – the person who leads an organization's board of directors.

describe – to tell about something with words or pictures.

disaster – an event that causes damage, destruction, and often loss of life. Natural disasters include events such as hurricanes, tornadoes, and earthquakes.

donate – to give. Something donated is a donation.

engineering – the application of science and mathematics to design and create useful structures, products, or systems.

franchise – to grant someone the right to sell a company's goods or services in a particular place.

inventory – the quantity of goods or materials on hand.

master's degree – a college degree usually earned after earning a bachelor's degree and studying two additional years.

PhD – doctor of philosophy. Usually, this is the highest degree a student can earn in a subject.

signature – something that sets apart or identifies an individual, group, or company.

software – the written programs used to operate a computer.

supermarket – a large store that sells foods and household items.

tangy – having a sharp taste or smell.

version – a different form or type of an original.

wok – a bowl-shaped pan that is used especially for cooking Chinese food.

Online Resources

Booklinks
NONFICTION
NETWORK
FREE! ONLINE NONFICTION RESOURCES

To learn more about Peggy Cherng, visit **abdobooklinks.com**. These links are routinely monitored and updated to provide the most current information available.

Index